The Narwhal's Tusk

Written by Carla Heymsfeld
Illustrated by Xiaojun Li

OWL'S HOUSE PRESS

L ong ago, when people believed magic unicorns roamed the forests of Europe, there lived a young sea captain. He was a handsome and clever man, but not altogether honest.

One day, when a summer storm forced his ship far north, he found himself in the cold waters of the Arctic. Curious about the strange ocean with its great hulks of floating ice, the captain cast his nets to see what he might find.

He could not believe his good fortune when he drew forth a whale, the one we call a narwhal. Never before had he seen such a creature. The whale's long ivory tusk looked exactly the way people imagined the horn of the unicorn.

A crafty look came upon the sea captain's face as his greedy fingers traced the magnificent ivory spiral. "My fortune is made," he said to himself. Drawing his sword, he cut off the poor whale's tusk and tossed him, alive but disfigured, back into the frozen waters of the ocean.

As soon as the ship sailed into port, the captain hurried to the castle of a wealthy old nobleman. He told the old man that the narwhal's tusk was the horn of a unicorn.

The nobleman, like most people of his time, believed unicorn horns had powerful magic that would make an old man feel young and strong again. He eyed the false prize hungrily as he listened to the captain's lies, and was only too glad to buy the narwhal's tusk for five times its weight in gold.

"Can you get me another?" the old nobleman then asked. "One I can make into a tall cup." In those days, people believed that a cup made from a unicorn's horn would sweat if the drink in it were poisoned, and the noble knew he had many enemies who might try to harm him.

"It takes much courage and skill to catch a unicorn," the sly captain said.

"I'll pay you ten times the horn's weight in gold," the noble promised.

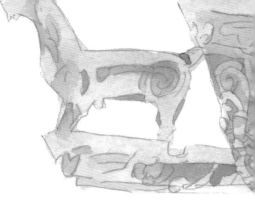

So the sea captain sailed again to the cold waters of the Arctic where he captured another narwhal. He brought the whale's beautiful tusk to the nobleman, who had it crafted into the tallest, most elegant cup in all of Europe.

But the noble was not yet content. "Bring me one more unicorn horn," he begged, "one I can grind into powder." Powder made from the horn of a unicorn was thought to be a wonderful medicine that could cure any disease.

"It is not easy to catch a unicorn," the sea captain reminded him.

"Bring me this horn and I will ask nothing more," the noble begged. "For your troubles I will pay you twice as much as before and give you my daughter's hand in marriage."

The sea captain was pleased. The noble's daughter was as beautiful as her father was rich, and during his visits to the castle they had learned to love each other. So, once again he sailed north to the Arctic, and once again he captured a narwhal. He brought the whale's tusk to the nobleman, and together they ground it into powder.

The nobleman was true to his word. Two days after the third tusk was delivered, the captain and the noble's daughter celebrated their wedding feast.

Years passed, and the sea captain prospered. He loved his wife and the children they had together.

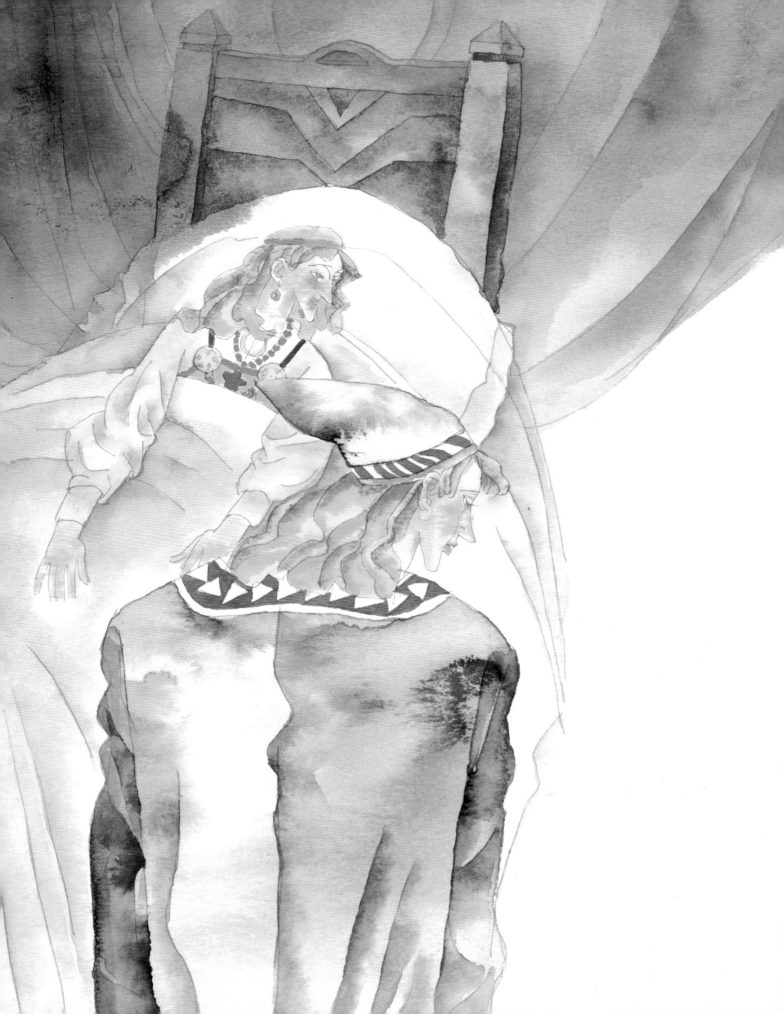

Then one day his wife became ill. The sea captain wanted to summon a doctor, but her father would not allow it. "We will use the magic of the unicorns," the old nobleman said. "We will place the magic horn at her head and give her some of the magic powder from the magic cup."

The sea captain was sick at heart, for he knew there was no magic in the whales' tusks. He watched his wife become weaker and paler as she drank the false medicine. When it seemed certain she would die, he knew he had to tell the truth. He knelt before the old man, and he made his confession.

The nobleman was very angry. Picking up the narwhal's tusk, the pouch of powder, and the cup, he threw them out the door and the captain after them.

Alone and grief stricken, the sea captain walked to the edge of the sea, where he sat upon the rocky shore and wept. He was there for a long time, and after a while, he had no more tears. As the night was dark and the rhythm of the waves was soothing, he soon fell into a deep sleep.

Suddenly, a voice called from the sea. "So, Captain," it said, "now you are tossed into the world as you once tossed us into the sea."

The startled captain peered into the black ocean. Floating before him were the three disfigured narwhals. "Is this possible?" he wondered aloud.

"Do you think your eyes and ears are as deceitful as your tongue?" the whale asked. Ashamed, the captain hid his head in his hands.

"You have lied and you have been cruel. Look how we have suffered because of your greed."

"I'm sorry," the captain said, stretching his arms toward the whales. "I would give anything if only I could undo the trouble I have caused."

"You say that now that you have nothing left to give." The whale's voice was stern.

"I have my life," the captain said. "I could give you that."

"No. We would not ask so high a price. That you repent and wish to atone is enough. We will help you." The whale inclined his head toward the long ivory tusk the captain had tossed on the rocks.

"Take my tusk into the center of the forest. Stab it into the ground. From this wound in the earth, there will come a spring."

The captain picked up the tusk and made ready to obey, but the whale's voice continued.

"That is not all. You must also sprinkle upon the earth the powder you have ground. Make a path into the forest, and you will see what you will see."

The sea captain tucked the pouch of powder into his belt, and the whale spoke again.

"When the time is right, fill the tall tusk cup with the water of the spring and give it to your wife." And with those words, the three whales turned and disappeared into the ocean.

The sea captain did not understand all the narwhal said, but having nothing to lose and everything to gain, he went in search of the center of the forest. He came to the spot just before midnight.

Grasping the tusk of the first whale, he stabbed it into the earth and a spring bubbled up as the whale said it would. Then, wasting no time, he sprinkled the powder, making a path into the forest. He watched to see what he could see and did not have long to wait.

A unicorn stepped out of the forest and danced along the glowing path. He dipped his spiraling horn into the spring and immediately the water ran clear and pure.

The sea captain knelt at the spring and filled his cup with the water. When he was finished, the unicorn was gone. All that remained were some sparkles on its magic path. The captain followed the tiny beacons and within minutes he was at his wife's bedside.

She was still as death. The captain wet her lips with water from the cup. A few minutes later she stirred, and again he brought the water to her mouth. All through the night he offered her water from the unicorn's spring, and by morning she was better.

Learning of his daughter's recovery, the grateful old nobleman crept into her room and stood by her bed next to the sea captain. The beautiful woman smiled to see them there together. "Love is the true magic," she whispered, gaining strength in the very breathing of the words.

The sea captain was never sure what happened that night. How much was a dream and how much was real? He kept the cup until the end of his days, however, and he never lied again.

For Sarah Anne, who brought magic into our lives.

– C.H.

For Huanhuan and Fei.

– X.L.

THE NARWHAL'S TUSK

ISBN: 1-891992-03-1
Library of Congress Number: 00-103628
First Edition

9 8 7 6 5 4 3 2 1

Owl's House Press
4966 El Camino Real, Suite #118
Los Altos, CA 94022
HYPERLINK http://WWW.OWLSHOUSE.COM   WWW.OWLSHOUSE.COM

We accept telephone orders at 1-888-848-OWLS